MAHATMA GANDHI

by Michael Nicholson

FOREWORD

Mohandas Karamchand Gandhi is one of the most fascinating of history's great men. He did not start life with any special advantages. But at a very early age he made a rule for himself — that he would act in accordance with truth. And he took a vow — never to be pushed around. All of us make such resolves, but we break them easily. He stuck to them. He also decided that he would not use violence, even if others used it against him. Through insistence on truth and non-violence and also active opposition to injustice, he developed enormous power within himself. He attracted large numbers of followers. His example unlocked the power within them. It is said that he made heroes out of dust. This happened first in South Africa, where he went as a young lawyer and where he fought against racial discrimision. After he returned to India twenty years later, the entire people of his motherland ranged behind him as if he was a Pied Piper. They hailed him as Mahatma, or the Great Soul. He led them to freedom from colonial rule.

Mahatma Gandhi was a saint who was active in the world's affairs. He was a man of religion who preached equal respect for all faiths. He disavowed any new message and claimed that what he said was as old as the hills. He also insisted that what he did, others could do. He wanted people to accept his path only if they were convinced it was right. When his country became free he held no office or position. He owned no property. His wealth was the love he gave and got from the people. He was full of laughter and fun. In the midst of his battle against an empire, he had time to share the cares and pains of the humblest. He was totally unafraid of death. And when he was killed by a fanatic, he had the name of God on his lips.

This book should enable young readers to understand how Mahatma Gandhi helped the world.

New Delhi
December 24, 1987

Rajiv Gandhi
Prime Minister of India

Picture Credits

BBC Hulton Picture Library — 31, 42; Camera Press — 12, 26, 58, 59; Tom Hanley — 24, 25, 44, 52, 61; Indo-British Films Ltd. — 20-1, 28-9, 32, 36-7, 40, 53, 57; the MacQuitty International Photographic Collection — 6 (top); National Army Museum — 15 (both), 30; National Gandhi Museum, New Delhi — 11, 13, 16, 19, 38 (below), 54, 56; Ann and Bury Peerless Slide Resources and Picture Library — 6 (below); the Photo Source — 4, 17, 43, 50, 55; Paul Popper Ltd. — 38 (top), 48, 51; the Royal Commonwealth Society — 9 (both), 10; BK Sinha — 49. The map on page 62 is reproduced by kind permission of the Press Information Bureau, Government of India.

Our grateful thanks go to Sir Richard Attenborough and Indo-British Films Ltd. for permission to reproduce stills from the film *Gandhi*.

North American edition first published in 1988 by
Gareth Stevens, Inc.
7317 W. Green Tree Road
Milwaukee, WI 53223 USA

Library of Congress Cataloging-in-Publication Data

Nicholson, Michael
    Mahatma Gandhi: the man who freed India and led the world in nonviolent change.
    (People who have helped the world)
    Includes index.
    Summary: Follows the life of the statesman who was a key figure in India's fight for independence from Great Britain.
    1. Gandhi, Mahatma, 1869-1948 — Juvenile literature 2. Nationalists — India — Biography — Juvenile literature. 3. Statesmen — India — Biography — Juvenile literature. [1. Gandhi, Mahatma, 1869-1948. 2. Statesmen] I. Title. II. Series.
DS481.G3N49 1988 954.03'5'0924 [B][92] 88-2098
ISBN 1-55532-813-X (lib. bdg.)
ISBN 1-55532-838-5

Series conceived and edited by Helen Exley.
Picture research: Diana Briscoe.
Research assistant: Margaret Montgomery.
Series editor, U.S.: Rhoda Irene Sherwood.
Editorial assistant, U.S.: Mary Thomas
Additional end matter, U.S.: Ric Hawthorne.

Printed in Hungary

MAHATMA GANDHI

The man who freed India and led
the world in nonviolent change ~~924197~~

by Michael Nicholson

8100737

~~6880~~

Gareth Stevens Publishing
Milwaukee

The watershed

None of us likes to feel unwanted. Even less do we like to take insults and abuse from others. In South Africa, Mohandas Gandhi was rapidly made aware that Indian people were disliked, unwanted, and frequently insulted. Barbers refused to cut his hair. He was not allowed to stay in white hotels. He was attacked and beaten up by a stagecoach driver when he refused to give up his seat to a white passenger.

Shortly after his arrival on a business visit to South Africa, Gandhi was put off a first-class railroad coach by a policeman acting at the request of a white passenger who refused to share a compartment with a brown-skinned Indian.

After being made to give up the seat for which he had a valid first-class ticket, Gandhi had to spend the night shivering in a freezing station waiting room. That night, he had plenty of time to consider his future as a new arrival in an unfriendly country. He had three options open to him. He could choose to ignore the insults and abuse and carry on regardless. Or he could go back to India as planned. Or he could decide to stay and fight racial prejudice. Gandhi decided to stay and use his legal knowledge to fight for the black people of South Africa.

Gandhi described this early experience in South Africa as a watershed — a turning point in his life. He was a changed man, a man who was born to change history. Now when we look back on his life, we can say it must surely have been a good thing that Gandhi was forced to endure the hardship and humiliation that so many of his fellow countrymen experienced all their lives. These experiences of injustice turned the shy young Indian lawyer (he was only twenty-four at the time) into a passionate fighter

"It has always been a mystery to me how men can feel themselves honored by the humiliation of their fellow beings."
Mahatma Gandhi,
in South Africa

5

Gandhi's tomb with the Hindi
inscription "Hey Rama," the words
Gandhi uttered as he died. In English,
the nearest translation is "Oh God."

Right: Mahatma Gandhi's statue
outside the house where he was born
in Porbandar, India. There are
statues and memorials throughout the
land in memory of the man regarded
by most Indians as their greatest
leader and saint.

6

for human dignity and freedom. For the next fifty years, he was to fight injustice not with weapons but with words and ideas, example and self-sacrifice. He developed *satyagraha*, a method of highly disciplined nonviolent civil disobedience. In South Africa and later in India, he taught his followers to face the British guns, bayonets, and *lathi* (steel-tipped poles), with highly organized, unarmed passive resistance. When the protesters, including thousands of women, were attacked and brutally beaten, they did not strike back. The people believed they were making fair demands of those in power, and they were prepared to break unjust laws and go to jail by the thousands.

His teachings were to spread from South Africa to India and eventually throughout the world. And after his death, they still give people deprived of freedom and justice a way to fight oppression without having to kill. Martin Luther King, Jr., Greenpeace, and other peaceful protesters all over the world — today we take their methods of demonstrating and applying pressure as the obvious ways to fight wrong. Before Gandhi, the only successful way people knew to fight oppression was to organize a fighting force.

By the time of his death, Gandhi had led the Indian nation to independence. Hitler had not been able to beat Great Britain's Churchill — but Gandhi had! This gentle, smiling man was revered by hundreds of millions of Indians, but also by the leaders of the rest of the world. The United Nations, in an un-precedented move, halted its deliberations when the news of his death reached New York. They recognized that here was a rare man. They recognized that here was a man whose influence would last far beyond his lifetime. He had given a new tool to all oppressed people across the world. It was a weapon of love, not of death.

The much-respected Albert Einstein said, "It may be that in years to come men will scarce believe that one such as this ever in flesh and blood walked upon this earth."

"Persons in power should be very careful how they deal with a man who cares nothing for sensual pleasure, nothing for riches, nothing for comfort or praise, or promotion, but is simply determined to do what he believes to be right."
Prof. Gilbert Murray,
Hibbert Journal, *1918*

"To observe at first hand that mighty effort, to rub up against, if ever so briefly, the towering greatness, the goodness, the high spirits and humor, the humility, the subtlety of mind, the integrity and purity of purpose, and that indefinable thing, the genius, of this man was the greatest stroke of fortune that ever befell me."
William L. Shirer,
Pulitzer Prize-winning
author of The Rise and Fall
of the Third Reich

7

Child of the Raj

Mohandas Karamchand Gandhi was born at Porbandar in India on October 2, 1869. In those days, the British ruled India. There were already more than 200 million people living in India, a population the States did not reach until 1970.

Gandhi was born into a land of contrasts — of desert plains, vast rivers, swamps, arid plateaus, dense jungles, and the highest mountain on earth. The climate of India is hot in the plains and cool in the highlands, but the vastness of India creates contrasts. India's people were separated from each other not only by the sheer difficulty of getting from one region to another, but also by different habits, religions, and over 300 languages. Even peoples of the same race and religion were divided one group from another by their caste or station in life.

The British had been in India since the early seventeenth century when they set up trading posts by force, bribery, or agreement with the Mogul Emperor and the local princes.

The British ruled over many races — black-skinned people in the south, as well as brown-skinned and pale-skinned people in the north. This was a land of princes and princelings, a land of great poverty and hunger and of vast riches. In India, those who were rich had to do nothing for themselves. There was always a servant to wash them, shave them, pour them a cool drink, or fan them when they were hot.

There were many different religions in India. Most people were Hindus, though of many different sects. The second largest group was the Muslims, whose prophet was Mohammed and whose book was the Koran. The Buddhists took their teachings from the Buddha, who lived 2,500 years ago. A very old Christian Church, whose faith was first brought to India by St. Thomas, worshipped according to an ancient rite. Ancient communities of Jews had been in India for many centuries. In the hills and forests were primitive tribal peoples. There were also the Parsees, who had originally come from Persia and

Opposite: The India Gandhi grew up in was the India of the British Raj, with all its pomp, grandeur and ceremony. The British brought great organization and technical progress to India, but they were all too often insensitive to the people they ruled.

Top: The British King, George V, firing over the head of an elephant at a tiger in the grass, in 1911. His total kill was 24. His party killed 39 tigers, 18 rhinoceros and 4 bears.

Bottom: This is another photograph of the kind of India Gandhi experienced as a young man. It shows ceremonial mace-bearers in scarlet and gold livery at a Delhi durbar ceremony held during British rule.

8

9

who worshipped fire as a symbol of God.

Hindu peasants, who were mainly vegetarians, worshipped the cow. Muslims, some of whom would eat beef, regarded pig meat as unclean. A sect called the Jains, who covered their mouths in case they swallowed a fly, would not go out at night for fear of treading on a worm. The white hunter, meanwhile, who could well have been a devout Christian, took delight in hunting the graceful tiger, almost to the vanishing point.

In 1869, the year of Gandhi's birth, the ties between Britain and India drew closer. The Suez Canal was opened, and British ships no longer had to sail all the way around Africa to reach India. The grip of British power on India had tightened. The links of trade had been made even stronger. Because Britain had colonies over most of the world, it used to be said "The sun never sets on the British Empire"; it seemed then that the Empire might last forever. Yet by the time of Gandhi's death seventy-eight years later, Britain had relinquished control of India. The gentle Gandhi was to play a great part in events leading to India's independence.

European "gentlemen" had servants who saw to all individual needs. The pay was 30 cents a month — less than half the wage for a similar position in England. This early photograph was taken in 1850 and shows a man being shaved by his personal servant.

Boy bridegroom

Mohandas Gandhi was his father Karamchand's fourth and last child. Mohandas was born into the *Vaisyu* caste, which ranked number three out of four in Hindu society, below the most respected *Brahmins* (or priests) and the *Kshatriyas*, (the soldiers or rulers). Still his caste was much more privileged than the *Sudra* (worker) caste. Below them all were those who had no caste, the Untouchables or "outcasts." These were the people who carried out the most unpleasant, dirty tasks in Hindu society — like cleaning the latrines. They were considered to be so low that caste Hindus thought they would be tainted if even their shadow fell on an Untouchable. These were the people Gandhi later called the *Harijan* or "children of God."

Gandhi was a normal boy from a happy Hindu family, occasionally mischievous but no more than

Gandhi at the age of seven. His mother, Putlibai, who was deeply religious, taught him the principles that marked his whole life.

most. His father was a court official and became the first Minister of the small princely state of Porbandar. His mother, Putlibai, was a very religious Hindu who prayed at each meal, fasted often, regularly visited the temple, and did not care for luxuries and jewels. Gandhi would later become India's greatest spiritual leader, and it was his mother's religious life that influenced him in these early years.

There were books at home and life was comfortable enough. The whole family were strict vegetarians, but Gandhi was once persuaded by a Muslim boy to eat goat meat. The boy told Gandhi that meat would make him grow tall and strong — strong enough to push the Englishmen out of India! In the mistaken belief that he would grow stronger, Gandhi tried eating goat meat. It gave him horrible nightmares, and he later deeply regretted it.

Gandhi was a shy boy. He would often run home

from school so that he did not have to speak to anyone. "I was always afraid lest anyone should poke fun at me," Gandhi remembered later. He loved taking long walks on his own and did not enjoy playing games.

When he was thirteen years old and still at school, Mohandas was married to Kasturba, the daughter of a Porbandar merchant. He had not been consulted about the marriage. As was the custom, and still is today in much of India, the parents of the young couple made all the arrangements, and the bride and groom did not meet until the wedding. We may wonder how such a marriage could have a chance of success, but for Mohandas and Kasturba it didn't seem strange. Their marriage lasted sixty-two years and produced four sons.

Student in the heart of empire

In 1888, at the age of nineteen, Gandhi set out on the three-week voyage to London, where he was to study law. He was already a father — Harilal, his first son, had been born some months earlier. His student days were not particularly happy; he felt lonely, cut off from his family, and distant from his spiritual home. He had sworn that while in London he would touch neither wine nor women and would keep to his strict vegetarianism. Gandhi's strict principles cut him off from many of his fellow students, making him feel more isolated.

Later he wrote, "I would continually think of my home and country. . . . Everything was strange . . . the people, their ways and even their dwellings. I was a complete novice in the matter of English etiquette and had continually to be on my guard." His vegetarian diet made things even more difficult, for many foods contained meat, and "Even the dishes [he] could eat were tasteless and insipid."

Still, like most people, Gandhi wanted to fit in as much as possible, so he went through a period of dressing in the fashion of the time. A fellow student recalled meeting Gandhi in Piccadilly Circus in London in 1890. Gandhi was "wearing a high silk top hat burnished bright, a stiff and starched white collar, and a rather flashy tie that displayed all the shades of the rainbow, under which there was a fine striped silk shirt. He wore as his outer clothes a morning coat, a double-breasted waistcoat and dark striped trousers to match. . . . He also carried leather gloves and a silver-mounted stick."

This is quite a contrast to the Gandhi the world came to know, the famous image of Gandhi dressed in simple sandals, a shawl, and his *dhoti*, a loincloth of homespun fabric.

After two years and eight months in England, Gandhi passed his final examinations at the Inner Temple Inn of Court in London and was called to the bar in June 1891. At just twenty-two years of age, he

Gandhi as a young man, dressed in elegant European clothing. During his time at the university in London, he did not wear Indian national dress. It was more than ten years later that he again took to Indian-style dress. And then he would dress as a holy man, in simple peasant garb.

had successfully completed his studies in French, Latin, physics, and Common and Roman Law. No doubt these studies helped train his mind. But though able and quick-witted, the young lawyer who sailed back from England did not yet show the wisdom and resourcefulness that was to inspire millions. He did not look as though he would free the largest nation in the British Empire and inspire millions of people. He himself referred to his college days as "the time before I began to live."

A new life in South Africa

On his return to India, Gandhi learned to his great sorrow that his mother had died. Gandhi had adored his mother, and she had had a considerable spiritual influence on him. Inspired by her religious belief, Gandhi developed his own reverence for all forms of life and his teachings on pacifism and nonviolence.

For nearly two years, Gandhi tried to establish himself as a lawyer in Bombay. The law practice was unsuccessful. He was given only one brief, and when he stood up in court to argue a case, he became so nervous he was unable to speak. He sat down to the sound of laughter in the courtroom. Shortly after this, Gandhi was offered the opportunity to represent a wealthy Indian merchant in South Africa, an opportunity that changed the whole of the rest of his life. He left to cover a single assignment, but was to stay for twenty-one years.

Then, as now, South Africa was a deeply divided society. Black people outnumbered the whites by more than five to one. The whites were themselves divided, and, during Gandhi's time in South Africa, they were to fight a bitter civil war. As a community, the 100 thousand or so Indian people in South Africa were despised. They had been imported to do lowly and disagreeable jobs that the black people would not do — mainly work on farms and grow sugar cane. These poor Indians, driven from home by semi-starvation, worked hard and lived in stinking, wretched poverty. However, a few prospered and began to compete with the whites, and for this they

SPION'S KOP
NATAL
JAN 24TH 1900

15

Gandhi with the Indian Ambulance Corps in the Boer War, 1899. He served with distinction and led a thousand ambulance men. He and his followers believed this gesture of support for the British would mean the Indians would receive better treatment. They were wrong.

became hated and feared. Numerous government rules and laws were made attacking the Indians and removing their rights to vote, own land, and move around freely.

Gandhi, whose resolve was stiffened by his own experiences of racial injustice in his early days in South Africa, soon became a leader of the Indian community. By 1896, he was also a rich and successful lawyer earning more than $450.00 a year, worth over $185 thousand in today's values!

How then did Gandhi help his people? Many of his ideas were practical. He set about making the Indians appear to be good people, more likeable, less strange to other people. He urged honesty in business so that they would be trusted. He taught cleanliness and sanitation. He advised them to learn English so that they could talk to the British. He urged them to drop their ideas about caste, which separated one group from another.

On a trip back to India in 1896 to fetch his family, he published *The Green Pamphlet,* which detailed Indian grievances in South Africa. This aroused much anger, and when he returned to South Africa in January 1897, he was attacked by a lynch mob. Later that year, under pressure from London, the legislature of Natal, a province in South Africa, repealed the laws allowing racial discrimination in electoral rights. They then replaced it with an educational test.

Despite the fact that Gandhi was a pacifist, a man of peace, he taught that the Indians should accept the obligations of nationality. If the Indians wanted the rights of citizens of the Empire, they must accept the obligations of citizens of the Empire. During the Boer War in 1899, although Gandhi sympathized with the Boers, he urged the Indian community to support the British. He helped to form and train an Indian Ambulance Corps. He led a thousand ambulance men, who served with distinction.

In December 1902, Gandhi presented the Indian community's grievances to Joseph Chamberlain, the Colonial Secretary. Both Natal and the Transvaal,

Gandhi, with some of the staff he employed at his firm in Johannesburg, South Africa. Gandhi had a profitable business and became very wealthy indeed. He was much admired by the South African Indian community because he was a highly educated lawyer, with a degree obtained in London.

another South African province, were doing their best to drive the Indian community out. An Asiatic Department was set up in the Transvaal in 1903 and produced a stream of new rules and regulations over the next three years. Tension grew between Indians and whites but went into abeyance during the Zulu Campaign of 1906. Again, Gandhi offered his help to the government and organized another Indian Ambulance Corps. Marching up to forty miles a day, they had to nurse a succession of flogged and wounded Zulus, a tribal people from Africa whom the white doctors and nurses would not touch!

The first struggles

In August 1907, the feelings of injustice in the Indian Community came to a head. The Black Act required that all Indian men and women register and be fingerprinted. Anyone without a certificate could be imprisoned, fined, or deported. The Indians called these Black Laws because they were aimed only at black, brown, and yellow people from Asia. Gandhi, though himself light brown in appearance, would often describe himself as black.

The Indian community was well aware of what the whites in South Africa intended to do. At an election meeting in January 1907, General Botha had declared, "If my party is returned to office we will undertake to drive the coolies [Indians] out of the country within four years."

It was at this time that Gandhi first articulated the idea of *satyagraha*, meaning "truth-force" or "love-force," which is "the vindication of truth not by the infliction of suffering on the opponent but on one's self." It requires self-control because one does not use violence against an opponent. Instead, the opponent must be "weaned from error by patience and sympathy." It is much more than passive resistance because it requires constant positive interaction between opponents as they move toward reconciling differences. He made strict rules as to how *satyagrahis*, people using *satyagraha*, should behave, and trained his people during the South African passive resistance campaigns. There was to be no retaliation for insults, floggings, or arrests. These were to be borne patiently. The idea was to humiliate opponents, not to beat them, but to melt their hearts.

In January 1908, because he had deliberately refused to register under the new law and had urged thousands of others to defy registration, Gandhi was sent to jail for two months. This was to be the first of many periods of imprisonment. He did not complain and was grateful to be given time for peaceful thoughts and reading. In fact, he served only one month of the sentence.

To test the unjust laws on immigration, many Indians crossed the Transvaal borders illegally. Gandhi did so and was jailed twice more. Whenever the Indians felt they were being treated as second-class citizens, they quietly refused to cooperate and

Kasturba, three Gandhi sons, and a nephew. This photograph was taken about 1903; the Gandhis would finally have four sons. Kasturba could not read or write, and she seemed to understand little of Gandhi's sophisticated and demanding course in life. Theirs was not a marriage of minds, yet they were very close, and she stayed by his side and supported him in all he did.

accepted their punishment.

In early 1913, General Smuts, a South African white leader, went back on a promise to repeal oppressive taxes and the ban on Indian immigration. Then a judge in the Cape Colony ruled that only Christian marriages were legal; all Indian wives thus became mistresses without any rights. For the first time, many women became involved in the civil disobedience campaign. The illegal border crossings into the Transvaal began again, and a group of women, called the Natal Sisters by Gandhi, was arrested. Other Indian women from the Transvaal then made their way to Newcastle, in Natal, where they persuaded the Indian miners to lay down their tools and go on strike. Many thousands of Indians were arrested and sent to jail, and as the word spread, thousands more went on strike.

Gandhi led his people into the Transvaal, and in four days he was arrested three times and finally imprisoned for three months. Gandhi, as usual, was happy to go to jail, for as he put it, "The real road to ultimate happiness lies in going to jail and

undergoing suffering there in the interests of one's own country and religion."

By the time Gandhi called off the *satyagraha* campaign, he was known and respected throughout South Africa and India. The lawyer who had once been unable to speak in court was a famous statesman known for his honesty, skill, and courage.

And so, in June 1914, Gandhi and Smuts eventually came together and worked out a give-and-take agreement that gave the Indian community more dignity and self respect. Gandhi's campaign of civil disobedience had triumphed, the first such campaign that would ever triumph.

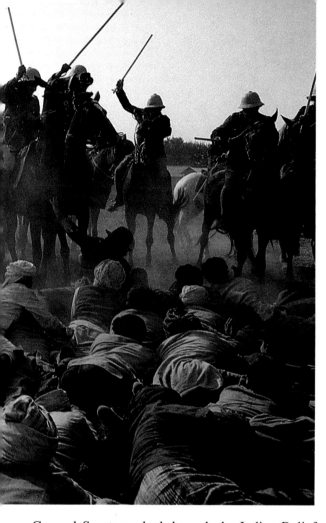

Gandhi led striking miners, who were charged by British soldiers trying to disperse them. Gandhi told the men to lie down, believing that horses could not be forced to trample on people. He was right. During this time in South Africa, Gandhi pioneered new methods of nonviolent civil disobedience, and at one time almost a quarter of the Indian people of the Transvaal were in prison.

General Smuts pushed through the Indian Relief Act, and at last, after twenty years, Gandhi felt free to return home. On parting, he sent General Smuts a pair of sandals he had made in prison. Smuts later said, "I have worn these sandals for many a summer since then, even though I may feel that I am not worthy to stand in the shoes of so great a man."

A fundamental change

It was during the twenty-one years of struggle in South Africa that Gandhi developed even more profound spiritual beliefs. He had always been a

Hindu, but now the great principles of the Bhagavad-Gita, the beautiful and powerful Hindu book of scripture, permeated his way of life.

His beliefs would from now on affect his politics, and they would be dominant in every political decision he would ever make. They also affected the way he dressed and the way he ate, indeed, every facet of his life.

It is difficult for non-Hindus to understand the principles Gandhi followed. Both in South Africa and later in India, the British would misjudge his habits as eccentric and faddish.

Gandhi was influenced by other religions and philosophies. He particularly liked Christian hymns and loved Christ's teachings. Christ's Sermon on the Mount, he said, "went straight to the heart." "Blessed are the meek," "Blessed be the poor for yours is the Kingdom of God," "Love your enemies." "Lay not up for yourselves treasures on earth" — these teachings of Christ were at the very heart of Gandhi's way of life.

He did not reject the other great religions and borrowed freely from the principles of other religious groups: Buddhists, Christians, Jains, Muslims. In fact partly because of this, he was seen as an unorthodox Hindu and was hated by strict Hindus. It was a strict orthodox Hindu who finally assassinated Gandhi because of his attempts to help the Muslims.

For Gandhi, one of the greatest principles, found in the Bhagavad-Gita, was called *samakhava*, which meant that people should not allow themselves to be upset by either pain or pleasure. They should work for the right without fear of failure or hope of success. Gandhi always laid as much stress on the means as on the end. He paid great attention to how to bring about change.

Another great principle he followed was *aparigraha* which involves rejecting material things. One could become spiritually rich by keeping life uncluttered, by not owning lots of goods. If you turn to the next page, you will see a picture of Gandhi's sum possessions at the time of his death.

"What did Gandhi teach me? I suppose the greatest single thing was to seek the truth, to shun hypocrisy and falseness and glibness, to try to be truthful to oneself as well as to others, to be sceptical of the value of most of life's prizes, especially the material ones, to cultivate an inner strength, to be tolerant of others. . . . "Also the necessity to discipline your mind and body and to keep your greeds and your lusts and your selfishness and your worldly ambitions in check; the obligation to love, to forgive and not to hate; to eschew violence and to understand the power of non-violence, grasping that the latter often demands more courage than the former."

Journalist *William L. Shirer, in* Gandhi, a Memoir

Ahimsa, or nonviolence to all living things, is another great principle of Hinduism. This means noninjury to everything that lives. And so Gandhi would not eat animals or hurt them. He hated all violence and would not even kill, or allow to be killed, the deadly snakes sometimes found in the grounds around his home in South Africa. He would guide them away with sticks.

But Gandhi's lasting legacy and most famous weapon was *satyagraha*, "truth force." Gandhi sought truth, rejecting anything hypocritical or false. He cultivated love and tolerance of other people and was himself usually loved and deeply respected by the people he opposed.

He was at peace because of his ability to meditate. Even when he was negotiating and working under great pressure — sleeping fewer than four hours a night — he was cheerful, smiling and joking, which may be why even his opponents came to love him.

He changed in South Africa, trying to discipline his body and mind and to check his greed, selfishness, and lust for any kind of bodily pleasure. He had, for example, become extremely successful and wealthy because of his legal skills. But he gave up all his wealth, including his home and fine clothes. He started an ashram, a communal farm similar to an Israeli kibbutz. He even tried to give away Kasturba's jewels, which satisfied wealthy clients had showered as gifts on the Gandhis. This was especially unpopular with her because by tradition the jewels would be needed as wedding gifts for her daughters-in-law.

There were many other sacrifices Gandhi demanded from his family and from his growing band of followers.

Gandhi and Kastuba came to a mutual decision to take the vow of *brahmacharya*. This means the complete cessation of all sexual activity. Gandhi felt that he had to rid himself of all physical desires in order to be at peace within himself and to be free under all circumstances to help others and to act with love at all times.

"I have not the shadow of a doubt that any man or woman can achieve what I have, if he or she would make the same effort and cultivate the same hope and faith."
Mohandas K. Gandhi

23

Gandhi's ashram at Sevagram, where spinning is part of daily prayers. All food is grown on the site, and the people lead a simple life of poverty. The Sevagram Ashram is still in operation.

So it was that during this period in South Africa, Gandhi's whole lifestyle changed. And the non-violent methods he pioneered and the political triumphs he was achieving were based on these deep spiritual beliefs.

His religion would be even more important in the coming struggle for freedom in India. The rise of Indian nationalism would go hand in hand with the increasing importance of Hinduism. Gandhi became the main instrument in both developments. Three-quarters of the Indian people were Hindu, and their religion had survived intact through wars, foreign conquest, and occupation. The Muslims had ruled India for centuries, but left Hinduism basically untouched. The large number of Christian missionaries had also made little impact. It was to be Gandhi's religious leadership coupled with his political craft that would enable him to bring freedom to India.

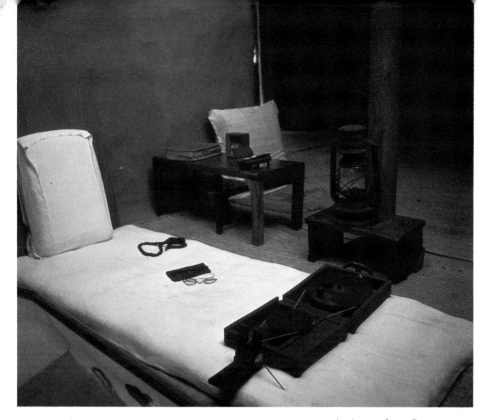

Gandhi comes home

In January 1915, when Gandhi was forty-five, he returned home. He and Kasturba, with their four young sons, were surprised to be met by huge crowds when they docked. Gandhi's achievements in South Africa were famous; and hundreds came to give him a warm welcome. The important people of Bombay held a grand reception to welcome him home.

Gandhi decided not to campaign for Indian rights until he had learned more about the problems in India. But he did set to work to establish his ashram at Sabarmati, near the city of Ahmedabad. The men and women of the community, eventually about two hundred of them, promised to live by Gandhi's rules. These were based on the religious principles he had taught himself to live by when he was in South Africa. Their lives were to be marked by honesty, truthfulness, celibacy, and poverty. They were to eat

A picture from Sevagram Ashram, showing Mahatma Gandhi's bed and belongings at the time of his death in 1948 — their value, $4.00. Gandhi's poverty and his way of life made personal criticism impossible for opponents. So it became a great political strength. It also made millions of Indian peasants feel that he was one of them and that he could lead and understand them.

25

Gandhi and Kasturba, soon after their return to India in 1915. Gandhi now went barefoot. He would never again don Western shoes or clothes.

a modest vegetarian diet. They were to lead a life of prayer and service to others.

You can imagine that ashram life could have become infuriating. All those rules! Saving paper and string and elastic bands. No luxuries. Yet Gandhiji* was such a warm, loving, charming person and his beliefs were so compelling that people wanted to be with him and live his way. From this time he would never be short of followers.

Gandhi rapidly became known as a champion of the people's rights. By 1917, people were calling him *Mahatma*, which means "great soul." He stuck up for the Untouchables, the poor peasants, and the poor factory workers in particular. Early in the year, he campaigned widely to abolish the practice of sending indentured workers to South Africa. Later the same year, he supported not only the Indigo sharecroppers in Bihar against their British landlords, but also the farmers of Gujarat against taxes, and the mill-workers of Ahmedabad in a strike against their employers. So influential did he become that later in 1917, in the darkest days of World War I, he was summoned to Delhi. The viceroy, who was the ruler of India, representative of the British, wanted Gandhi's assistance. To the great surprise of many pacifists, Gandhi agreed to call for Indian volunteers to fight for Britain and the Empire.

Gandhi still believed that Britain was a force for good. He also believed, as he had in South Africa, that if the Indian people wanted the rights of the citizens of Empire, they should serve the Empire if asked to do so.

So it was that volunteer Indian soldiers went to fight alongside British soldiers and soldiers from other nations controlled by Great Britain. The Indian soldiers fought in Mesopotamia and in Europe on the Western Front, and many died in this cruel and wasteful war.

The Great War, as it became known, was to alter the course of history. The British and their allies, including the United States, finally won, but at a tremendous cost. Britain was severely weakened.

*ji is added to the end of a name as a sign of affection and respect.

Although few thought so at the time, the days of the British Empire were numbered. The Indian soldiers knew they had earned the right to dignity, equality and self-respect. There was a new mood abroad.

Yet the Indian soldiers were to be disappointed. The half promise of self-government that Britain had given India during the war was not kept. Worse still, the emergency war powers and restrictions on liberties were to be kept on after the war. Trial without jury and imprisonment without trial were to be retained. The Indian people felt cheated.

The old insensitivity of the British that Gandhi had seen in South Africa was unchanged: the British had no intention at all of giving up their most popular and profitable colony.

> *"Europe has completely lost her former moral prestige in Asia. She is no longer regarded as the champion throughout the world of fair dealing and the exponent of high principle, but as the upholder of western race supremacy and the exploiter of those outside her own borders."*
> *Rabindranath Tagore, India's famous writer, who first called Gandhi the "Mahatma [Great Soul] in peasants' garb."*

The first campaign

For the first time, Gandhi decided to go against the British Government of India. He decided on a *hartal*, a kind of general strike. He proclaimed a day when no business was to be done. Stores were to stay shut. Employees were to strike. This began a twenty-eight-year struggle that would finally bring an end to British rule.

There was tremendous support for the *hartals* organized by Gandhi against the unjust laws. Unfortunately, public protest turned into rioting in Delhi, Ahmedabad, Lahore and Amritsar. Gandhi denounced the trouble-makers and called off the whole campaign. Gandhi saw that the people had to be trained in obedience before civil disobedience could work.

As a penance for the violence and rioting, Gandhi announced he would fast for seventy-two hours, and he called upon others to fast for twenty-four hours.

The Amritsar massacre

April 13, 1919, was India's blackest day. A forbidden meeting was held at Amritsar, the sacred city of the Sikhs, in a large open space surrounded on three sides by high walls and known as the Jallianwalla Bagh.

The local British Army Commander, General Dyer, decided to suppress the assembly with the utmost brutality. Without warning, he ordered a small force of native troops to fire into the unarmed crowd. There was no way to escape. The soldiers fired for ten minutes, leaving 379 people killed and more than 1,200 wounded.

At least some of the lives might have been saved if General Dyer had not refused to allow Indian medics in to tend to the wounded.

Dyer said later, "I thought I would be doing a jolly lot of good." To the Commission of Enquiry, he said, "Yes, I think it quite possible that I could have

At the Sikh's holy city of Amritsar, the crowds gathered for a demonstration in sympathy with Gandhi's nonviolent hartal. It was a religious festival, and the crowd of men, women and children were in a holiday mood. Without warning, the troops opened fire. Hundreds were killed. This was the turning point for Gandhi: from then on he would oppose the British head-on.

Scene from the film, Gandhi

924/47

dispersed them without firing, but I was going to punish them."

At Amritsar, General Dyer also enforced the Crawling Order. He ordered that in retaliation for an injury done against an English missionary woman, soldiers should be posted with fixed bayonets along the street where she lived. These soldiers were to ensure that all Indians crawled along the street on their bellies. It didn't matter if feeble old men and women had to pass down the street to reach their homes. Hundreds of Indians were made to crawl in the dirt and dust.

29

In June 1920, Gandhi returned the war medals he'd received in South Africa. He wrote to the British viceroy, "I can retain neither respect nor affection for a government which has been moving from wrong to wrong in order to defend its immorality."

Most Indians, Gandhi included, felt totally humiliated by this. And it was something they would never forget.

Many British people, though not all, were deeply ashamed of General Dyer's deeds and of his various attempts at Amritsar to punish and humiliate the Indian people. The shock waves from the bloody event spread through the whole of India. The effect of Dyer's cruelty was to strengthen opposition to British rule. It also brought Gandhi into politics in a way he had never before sought or wanted. "I had faith in them until 1919, but the Amritsar Massacre and other atrocities in the Punjab changed my heart." For the first time, he began to see that British rule had to be overthrown. He returned his two British war medals and took on the leadership of the Indian nationalist movement. He realized that mere self-rule and justice were not enough. The British had to leave India.

Congress reform

Before Gandhi joined it, the Indian National Congress was a group of middle-class windbags. Gandhi breathed new life into it and rapidly became its leader. He turned it into a mass democratic organization, with branches all over the country, even in the villages.

In December 1920, the Congress at Nagpur passed Gandhi's resolution calling for *swaraj*, or self-rule. If possible, they wanted to be like Canada and Australia, to have self-rule inside the British Empire. But they would go outside the Empire if necessary. The Muslim leaders wanted to remain within the Empire, and after the resolution was passed, they began to lose interest in the Congress. The Hindu and Muslim leaders started to drift apart.

At Nagpur, in 1920, the Congress called for the liberation of the Untouchables and for the revival of village industries. Gandhi hated the way the Untouchables were treated by the caste Hindus. He saw cruelty to the Untouchables as an insult and a threat to the Hindu religion. He wanted unity, unity based on equality.

Spinning for victory

The collapsible spinning wheel was to become an article of faith to Gandhi and his followers. Its gentle and relaxing hum could be heard at Congress meetings or wherever nationalists gathered together. The spinning wheel was to become the symbol of liberation. It was practical. It was affordable. It made use of hands that had nothing else to do.

Gandhi saw in the spinning wheel and home weaving a way to revive village economy and alleviate poverty. He attributed the desperate poverty of the Indian villages to the town dwellers and the British textile mills, which had destroyed the village craft industry. For the rest of his life, Gandhi would spin two hundred yards of yarn every single day. Even if he was at an an international conference or worked until two o'clock in the morning, he would not sleep until he'd spun his daily quota. He also wanted basic education for all and the use of Hindi as

As part of a boycott of British goods, Gandhi urged Indians to spin their own cloth. Every day Gandhi would spin two hundred yards of yarn. No matter how busy he was, he would never go to sleep until he had spun his daily quota.

Gandhi gave up the civil disobedience campaign after a group of his followers killed twenty-two policemen at Chauri Chaura. The demonstrators set fire to the police station, forcing the policemen out. They were hacked to death. This picture was a careful reconstruction of the event in the Gandhi *film.*

the national language.

Gandhi, as he said himself, "turned the spotlight all over." In these months of whirlwind activity, he turned to all kinds of problems. He was concerned with dirty streets, people's spitting, rudeness on trains, neglect of poor farmers and, above all, any kind of violence.

During 1921, Gandhi traveled throughout India in third-class railroad compartments, spreading the message that noncooperation would lead to independence. At vast public meetings, he urged the people to give up wearing foreign clothing and to boycott British cloth.

His followers would strip off their foreign-made clothes and throw them into a fire. Volunteers would picket stores selling British cloth. By this time, Gandhi himself had permanently adopted his famous loincloth and carried a homespun bag. Unfortunately, merchants' stocks of foreign clothing were also set afire, and flames from burning warehouses lit the sky at night. Gandhi did not approve of such actions.

In October 1921, a Congress working party called upon soldiers and civil servants to desert their posts. Lawyers were urged to give up their practices, and many did so. Schools and colleges were disrupted. More and more villages refused to pay taxes. By December, twenty thousand people had been imprisoned for civil disobedience and sedition.

The country was in a state of great excitement. Chaos was the order of the day. But amidst the fine expressions of pacifism and high ideals, there was growing disorder and violence in the streets. Even the British who knew India well were bemused and bewildered by the leading revolutionary activists. Especially by Gandhi — gentle Mr. Gandhi, middle-aged, dressed in a loincloth, always smiling his toothless smile, and by now attracting thousands of excited supporters wherever he went. They would walk for days just to see their great leader. As things came to a boil, rioting and disorder spread. Gandhi fasted as a penance for the violence. Then in February 1921, in the Chauri Chauru (United Provinces), twenty-two police constables were killed by an enraged mob during a campaign of mass disobedience. Gandhi was sickened by the atrocity and stopped the defiance of the government everywhere in India.

"It is better," said Gandhi, "to be charged with cowardice and weakness than to be guilty of denial of our oath and to sin against God. It is a million times better to appear untrue before the world than to be untrue to ourselves."

Many were disappointed, many felt let down, betrayed. But Gandhi was not prepared to sacrifice the principle of nonviolence.

The first stage of the struggle was at an end. What had it achieved? In the first place, Congress had flexed its muscles and demonstrated its power. There were hundreds of thousands of people prepared to make great sacrifices, to give up their jobs and risk

"I came reluctantly to the conclusion that the British connection had made India more helpless than she was before, politically and economically. India has become so poor that she has little power of even resisting famines. Before the British advent, India spun and wove in her millions of cottages just the supplement she needed for adding to her meager agricultural resources. This cottage industry, so vital to India's existence, has been mined by incredibly heartless and inhuman processes. The profits and the brokerage are sucked from the masses."
Mohandas K. Gandhi

imprisonment in the cause of freedom.

But it only convinced Gandhi that for non-violence to succeed, his supporters had to be highly trained and much more disciplined. He himself sought atonement for the murders in Chauri Chaura by going on a five-day fast.

For the British government of India it meant that Congress could no longer be ignored. The demands of Indian nationalism had to be recognized and in some way satisfied.

The nationalists themselves felt a new strength. They had got rid of their inferiority complex and felt able to deal with the government on equal terms.

Arrest and imprisonment

Shortly after the killings at Chauri Chaura, in March 1922, Gandhi was arrested. He was charged with rebellion against the government. At his trial, Gandhi, who described himself as a farmer and weaver, pleaded guilty. He made a long statement in which he said, "The section under which I am charged is one under which mere promotion of disaffection is a crime. I have studied some of the cases under it, and I know that some of the most loved of India's patriots have been convicted under it. I consider it a privilege, therefore, to be charged under that section. . . . I hold it to be a virtue to be disaffected toward a government which in its totality has done more harm to India than any previous system. India is less manly under the British rule than she ever was before. Holding such a belief, I consider it a sin to have affection for the system.

"I am here therefore to invite and submit to the highest penalty that can be inflicted upon me for what in law is a deliberate crime and what appears to me to be the highest duty of a citizen."

Gandhi did receive the maximum sentence of six years and went cheerfully to prison again. He told the trial judge he was grateful for the courtesy he had received during the trial. He had no regrets. "We must widen the prison gates," he said. "Freedom is to be wooed only inside prison walls." Happy in his prison cell, Gandhi spent his time at peace — reading his books, spinning his wheel, and saying his prayers. He was released in 1924 because of an operation for acute appendicitis.

When Gandhi came out of prison, he discovered that the Indian National Congress was in disarray. The noncooperation movement had collapsed. Even worse, there was much community unrest and bitterness between Muslims and Hindus. But Gandhi chose not to renew his campaign of civil disobedience until his prison sentence was served. Instead, he devoted much time in the next few years to trying to bring the two communities together.

In these quiet years, Gandhi carried on preaching the virtues of the spinning wheel and the handloom. Gandhi said the wheel was like a restful prayer. He was accused of homespun fanaticism. But he persisted. He said it was the great British textile mills and the Indian cities that had made the Indian countryside so poor. Gandhi urged his people to wear *khadi*, or homespun cloth. By buying *khadi*, the townspeople would help the peasants. Homespun was to be the link between town and country, rich and poor. The India of jewels and riches and silver and gold brocade was not Gandhi's India. Homespun became the badge of the nationalists and the Congress Party.

"I believe that I have rendered a service to India and England by showing in non-cooperation the way out of the unnatural state in which both are living. In my humble opinion, non-cooperation with evil is as much a duty as is cooperation with good."
Gandhi, speaking at his trial.

"It must be emphasized that nonviolent resistence is not a method for cowards; it does resist. If one uses this method because he is afraid or merely because he lacks the instruments of violence, he is not truly non-violent. This is why Gandhi often said that if cowardice is the only alternative to violence, it is better to fight."
Dr. Martin Luther King, Jr., "An Experiment in Love," Jubilee, September, 1958

Civil disobedience

In 1929, Gandhi, now aged sixty, turned again to freeing India. The new campaign of civil disobedience was to be different from the earlier campaign. Then, people had hoped to bring the government to a standstill by striking and pulling out of government jobs. That had failed, though it did give the government a nasty jolt at the time.

The new campaign encouraged people to break the law. The mass arrests that would follow would earn sympathy from many and gradually make government impossible.

Gandhi won the support of many doubters because of the sense of his position. He pointed out

that over eighty percent of Indians were peasants. To win their support, it was essential to speak their languages, dress like them, and understand their economic requirements and aspirations. They were far more likely to listen to an old man in a *khadi* loincloth and sandals who spoke their own language than they were to a Europeanized Congress member using English!

The new campaign started with a peaceful revolt against taxes. And it ended with a total victory for the peasants. Throughout 1929, Gandhi toured much of India, speaking at rallies and organizing bonfires of foreign cloth.

But Gandhiji had promised that he would declare himself "an Independence-*wallah*" if India did not achieve the same status as Canada or Australia by

December 31, 1929. Now he moved into action with his historic Salt March.

A pinch of salt

The climax to Gandhiji's much publicized Salt March was when he quietly stooped and picked up a handful of salt. This simple gesture was the end result of Gandhi's carefully planned and disciplined 24-day, 200-mile march. Now over sixty and looking frail, Gandhi had led his small band of seventy-eight followers from his Sabarmati Ashram to the sea. By the time they arrived, several thousand villagers had joined them. The British treated it as a joke and dismissed the whole idea. Why was there any drama about picking up a handful of salt? Once again they underestimated Gandhi. They had no understanding

Gandhi had waited years before he unleashed another civil disobedience campaign, for he knew what power he held over the Indian people. He knew, too, how dangerous a nonviolent campaign could be if discipline broke down. After carefully writing to the British viceroy to give him a chance to back down, Gandhi launched the great campaign. He and a band of followers walked slowly, very slowly, to the sea — to pick up a handful of salt!

Above: Gandhi on the Salt March.
He was with Mrs. Saronjini Naidu,
the poet and his close associate.
Gandhi was soon arrested, and Mrs.
Naidu led 2,500 protesters on the
world famous and fateful Dharasana
Salt Works demonstration (see
previous page).

Right: Gandhi stooped for a
handful of salt. This symbolic
gesture started a nationwide
outbreak of civil disobedience, as
hundreds of thousands of Indians
broke the law by producing
their own salt.

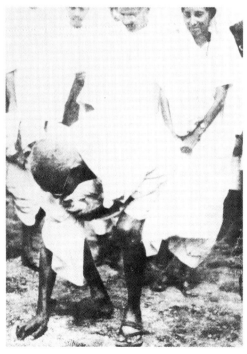

of the feelings now running in India, and they certainly had no understanding of how formidable and clever Mahatma Gandhi would be now that he was an outright opponent.

The idea behind the march was to inspire widespread civil disobedience to embarrass the government. The Salt Tax that Gandhi set out to destroy was not only a symbol of the government's right to tax and therefore its right to rule – it was an emotional issue. The tax bore hardest on the poor, for no one, particularly in a hot country, can live without salt. The poorest peasant was found to pay as much as the richest merchant. Many also thought that to tax a substance that nature provided free was especially repugnant.

Gandhi's flouting of the Salt Tax law gripped people's imaginations. Civil disobedience broke out in nearly every province. All over India, poor people began taking salt from the sea. At least sixty thousand people were arrested, including nearly all the Congress leaders.

On the night of May 5, 1930, Gandhi himself was arrested. He had been asleep under a mango tree near the seashore. The police came brandishing guns. Gandhi was quite calm and brushed his teeth with a twig in the Indian way before allowing himself to be taken off. There was no trial and no sentence. He was simply locked away.

Gandhi had relied on being arrested. It was all part of the strategy.

"As we saw the abounding enthusiasm of the people and the way salt-making was spreading like a prairie fire, we felt a little abashed and ashamed for having questioned the efficacy of this method when it was first proposed by Gandhi. And we marvelled at the amazing knack of the man to impress the multitude and make it act in an organized way."
Jawaharlal Nehru, leader of Congress and later India's first Prime Minister

Satyagraha in action

Protests continued after Gandhi's imprisonment. Mrs. Sarojini Naidu, the poet, led 2,500 Congress volunteers to the Dharasana Salt Works. This was defended by policemen armed with *lathi*. After prayers, the protesters moved forward. The first column was headed by one of Gandhi's four sons, Manilal. They were viciously attacked and beaten about the head by the soldiers. Obeying the rules of nonviolence, they did not defend themselves. They fell where they stood, as the sticks rained on their

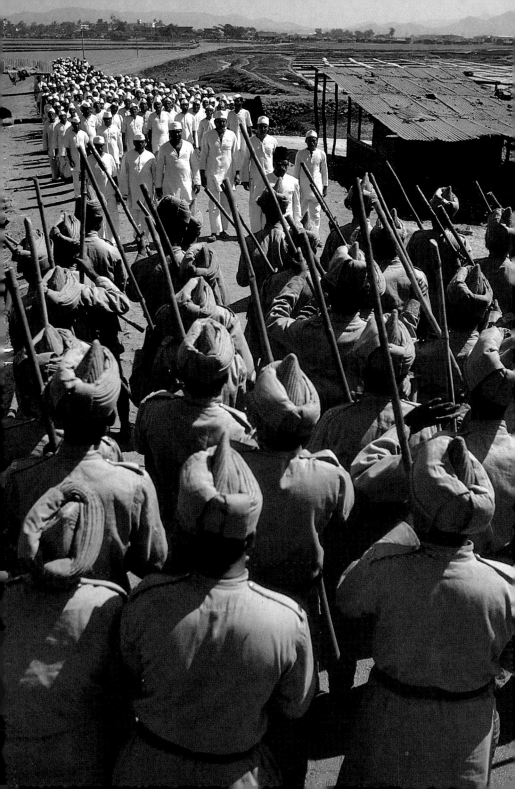

heads with sickening thuds. As the wounded fell with fractured skulls and concussions, they were dragged away by women protesters. A second column drew up and in complete silence approached the stockade. The British officer barked an order and the police beat the protesters down. They were dragged away.

A new column formed. As Webb Miller, a journalist for United Press, recounted later, "They marched steadily, with heads up, without the encouragement of music or cheering or any possibility that they might escape serious injury or death. The police rushed out and methodically and mechanically beat down the column. There was no fight, no struggle; the marchers simply walked forward till struck down."

Miller's account of the horror was published in more than a thousand newspapers. It did much to stir the conscience of Britain and the world about what was happening in India. Yet again, *satyagraha* was succeeding. The more unjust and cruel the British were, the more they played into Gandhi's hands.

Within a year, Gandhi, the "seditious *fakir,* * was striding half naked up the steps of the viceroy's Palace, there to negotiate and parley on equal terms with the representative of the King Emperor," to quote Churchill's angry comment.

The viceroy, Lord Irwin, and Gandhi trusted each other. Their negotiations resulted in the Irwin-Gandhi Pact. This was an agreement to, among other things, permit the free manufacture of salt. Civil disobedience was called off, prisoners were to be released, and Congress was to be represented at the Second Imperial Conference in London.

The round table conference

In August 1931, Gandhi sailed for Britain as the sole representative of the Indian National Congress. On embarkation, Gandhiji warned, "I might come back empty handed." He didn't hope for much from the

*A fakir is an Indian beggar monk

Opposite: The scene of the Dharasana Salt Works demonstration in the film Gandhi. *It shows exactly how the 2,500 Gandhi followers, dressed in white, assembled in groups. Each group faced the four-hundred Indian policemen who carried five-foot* lathi *with steel tips. Wave after wave of demonstrators would assemble and wait peacefully to be beaten senseless.*

"All hope of reconciling India with the British Empire is lost forever. I can understand any government taking people into custody and punishing them for breaches of the law, but I cannot understand how any government that calls itself civilized could deal as savagely and brutally, with nonviolent, unresisting men as the British have this morning."

V.J. Patel, leader of the swaraj (self-rule) during Gandhi's arrest.

Gandhi arriving at 10 Downing Street, London, the home of the British Prime Minister. His informal Indian peasants' dress caused a great deal of publicity. But the British leaders were astounded at Gandhi's negotiating skills and unflagging energy. Always smiling and happy, he drafted resolutions, delivered talks in public, and gave press interviews. He kept five secretaries busy and got only four hours' sleep a night.

Conference. In truth, he wasn't all that interested in the details of just how a new government should work. His was the human approach, and at the human level he scored a great success. He conquered the hearts of many British men and women and persuaded many more of the justice of his cause.

Newspaper headline writers loved him. When asked whether he had felt sufficiently clothed when he visited the King, he said, "The King had enough on for both of us." The English were intrigued by details of Gandhi's personal habits, his dress, his diet.

When he visited the cotton towns of Lancashire to explain his reasons for boycotting British cloth, the workers cheered, even though many were unemployed because of his policy. They liked the fact that Gandhi had taken the trouble to talk with them. This was something their own rulers rarely, if ever, did.

"Do you want your own prosperity to be built upon the misery of others?" Gandhi asked them. And they said, "No." He told them they were better off on their unemployment pay every week than an Indian worker who got less than half of that per *month* when he was working.

Gandhi was not a materialist. He did not mind being poor. But he did hate grinding, desperate poverty. Gandhi said, "No sophistry, no jugglery in figures, can explain away the evidence that the skeletons in many villages present to the naked eye. I have no doubt that both England and the town dwellers in India will have to answer, if there is a God above, for this crime against humanity which is perhaps unequalled in history. . . .

"My ambition is no less than to convert the British people through non-violence and thus make them see the wrong they have done in India. I do not seek to harm your people. I want to serve them even as I want to serve my own."

Gandhi's personal triumph was tremendous, but the conference itself was a failure. In fact, it was worse than a failure because it widened the differences between the Indians themselves. As

Gandhi put it, "They went into the conference Muslim and Sikhs and Untouchables, and they came out of it Muslims and Sikhs and Untouchables — and never at any moment was the Indian nation there."

And so Gandhi — dejected but determined — left for India. He never returned to Britain.

Children of God

Within three weeks of Mahatma Gandhi's return to India, he was back in jail. Once again, in prison he turned his attention to the Untouchables and began a fast to the death. His epic fast stirred the conscience of the people of India. Gandhi won some concessions from Congress about the way the Untouchables were to be elected. More importantly, the effect of his fast was to improve the lot of the *Harijan*. They were not only touched but even embraced by their fellow Hindus. Wells and temples where they had not been allowed to go were now

Hundreds of thousands of Lancashire cotton workers had become unemployed because of the boycott and burning of British cloth, which Gandhi had led. Yet he was welcomed by the unemployed people and spoke to them about the far worse poverty in India. His listeners immediately realized that Gandhi not only sympathized with their problems but also understood the workings of the cotton manufacturing industry.

43

A village of Untouchables in Maharashta, in western India. Gandhi thought that the caste system, and especially the treatment of the Untouchables, was the worst aspect of Hinduism. He campaigned on their behalf and almost died on a fast to the death for improvements in their way of life. Gandhi called them the Harijans which means "children of God."

thrown open to them.

After his release from prison in 1933, Gandhi set out on a twelve-thousand-mile *Harijan* tour, collecting money for the Untouchables.

Gandhi was a religious Hindu and believed that if you led a bad life, you would come back to earth as a member of an inferior caste. But Gandhi would not accept untouchability. As he said, "I know of no argument in favor of untouchability. . . . Indeed I would reject all authority if it is in conflict with sober reason or the dictates of the heart."

Gandhi's fight for the Untouchables was only partly successful. The fight still goes on. To this day, government officials and community leaders lead little bands of Untouchables into tea shops and

44

barber shops. Sometimes they are allowed back even when the officials have gone away again!

In these quiet years, Gandhiji took less direct action in Congress affairs and concentrated on welfare work. He also worked constantly on an issue that was central to him — Hindu-Muslim unity. The two groups were drifting further apart, and Gandhi was heartbroken. He could see that independence would probably cause the final split, and preferred to delay independence if that meant they could avoid that final rift.

Storm clouds of war

If there was ever any doubt that the British would be forced to leave India within a few years, the events of 1939 settled the matter. India was not prepared for war. The rise of Fascism in Europe had seemed a faraway threat. When war came, it had a dramatic impact on Asian thinking.

On the whole, India's Congress leaders supported Britain in her fight, but they resigned when, without consulting them, the viceroy decided that India was also at war. To try to win Congress over, the British promised independence after the war, but Gandhi insisted on independence at once. In spite of this, Gandhi was on the side of the Allies. He did not want to seize independence violently nor did he want to take advantage of Britain's difficulties. "We do not seek our independence out of Britain's ruin," he said.

In August 1942, Gandhi called upon the British to quit India. He told the All-India Congress Committee, "Our quarrel is not with the British people. We fight their imperialism." Perhaps Gandhi did not fully understand the significance of his action. Certainly he regretted the dreadful riots that followed his "Quit India" demand.

Kasturba's death

Violence broke out again all over India when, two days after his "Quit India" speech, Gandhi was arrested and imprisoned yet again.

"To see the universal and all-pervading spirit of truth face to face one must be able to love the meanest of creatures as oneself."
Gandhi, in his autobiography

"I hold myself to be incapable of hating any being on earth. By a long course of prayerful discipline, I have ceased for over forty years to hate anybody. I know this is a big claim. Nevertheless, I make it in all humility."
Mohandas K. Gandhi

This was a time of great personal tragedy for Gandhi. Within a few days of his arrest, his devoted secretary, Mahadev Desai, died suddenly. Then his wife became sick. Gandhi and Kasturba, whom he called Ba, spent the last months of their lives together in prison. Their relationship, which had often been difficult when they were young, had mellowed with age. Kasturba had come to be a significant influence on Gandhi's life, if only in the background. When death came, it was Gandhi who was holding her. Gandhi said, "I can say of the vacuum that has been created by Ba's death, it is something very different, a vacuum which cannot be filled." He and Ba had been together since childhood. She had borne Gandhi four sons.

Six weeks after his wife's death, Gandhi was released from prison. He was ill, and the viceroy feared more violence if he were to die in jail.

The transfer of power

The Allied Victory in 1945, at the end of World War II, marked the beginning of the end of colonialism. Britain was exhausted, and the new Labour government was committed to Indian independence.

The British in India knew that time was running out. The Indian Civil Service had not recruited an English person since 1939. The Civil Service in India was getting old, tired, and understaffed. It had had to deal with mounting food and cloth shortages, including a terrible famine in Bengal in 1943. Desperate poverty was widespread.

In 1945, the other Congress leaders were released from prison. In the elections that followed, Congress kept its position as the largest political party, but it no longer spoke for the Muslims. During the war, with Congress leaders in prison, the Muslim leader Mohammed Ali Jinnah and his Muslim League had gained increasing support for a Muslim state of Pakistan. Gandhi and Congress hated the idea of Partition, the division of India.

Britain's new Labour government decided to

make a last attempt to preserve Indian unity, and a cabinet mission was sent out to Delhi in 1946. Negotiations dragged on for three months and finally broke down because Congress and the Muslim League could not trust each other.

The viceroy then, Lord Wavell, invited a disciple of Gandhi, Jawaharlal Nehru, to form a temporary government. Nehru asked Jinnah for help in running the government and offered members of the Muslim League several government posts. But Jinnah was unable to agree.

In August, the Muslim League decided upon a Direct Action Day to protest against Congress government and to force the British to recognize their demand for a separate state. This led to a fearful outbreak of violence in the Calcutta region. Four thousand people were killed and fifteen thousand injured in a wave of shootings, stabbings and burnings. The bloodshed and murder spread to East Bengal. Muslim gangs roamed about forcibly converting Hindus or killing them.

The news horrified Gandhi who decided to go himself, vowing, "I intend to bury myself in East Bengal until such a time as the Hindus and Muslims learn to live together in peace. . . . I do not know . . . what I shall be able to do there. All that I know is that I won't be at peace unless I go."

Gandhi himself described his mission as the most difficult in his whole life. When a colleague went to visit Gandhi in East Bengal, he found him in the house of a *dhobi*, a village washerman: "So there he was in the little hut of the village washerman, writing his letters by the light of a kerosene lamp." People found it heartbreaking to see the frail little man, now seventy-seven-years-old, walking barefoot from village to village. But Gandhi threw every effort into his supreme task. He held prayer meetings. He received deputations. He preached courage, forgiveness and truth.

From Bengal, Gandhi went to Bihar, where the victims of the riots were Muslims rather than Hindus. By March, Gandhi was holding prayer meetings,

"The welcome was so disarming, his manner so friendly and radiant, that my nervousness evaporated before I could say a word. "His gray eyes lit up and sharpened when they peered at you through his steel-rimmed spectacles, and they softened when he lapsed, as he frequently did, into a mood of puckish humor. I was almost taken back by the gaiety in them. This was a man inwardly secure, who, despite the burdens he carried, the hardships he had endured, could chuckle at man's foibles, including his own."
William L. Shirer, in Gandhi a Memoir

An ugly riot in Bombay, showing a scene of communal Hindu-Muslim violence. Over half-a-million people were killed in the move to independence. Had it not been for Gandhi, the number of dead could have run into millions and a full-scale civil war would have developed.

trying to get Muslims back in their homes, and collecting money from Hindus for Muslim relief. He stayed in a small Muslim village, went on a partial fast, and vowed he would not leave until Muslims and Hindus were at peace. One month later, the killings stopped.

The last viceroy

The continuing disorder in India, despite the Mahatma's efforts, made the British Government fearful. Jinnah still held out for Partition, and the resolve of Congress was weakening. Despairing of reaching agreement and horrified at the prospect of civil war, British Prime Minister Clement Attlee made a bold decision: the British would hand over power no later than June 1948. The new and final viceroy appointed for the job was Lord Louis Mountbatten. In World War II, he had been England's Commander in Southeast Asia and was a cousin of Britain's King George VI. Mountbatten came to the job youthful, fresh, and informed, with complete authority. He arrived in Delhi in March 1947 and almost immediately sent word to Gandhi that he wished to see him.

Mountbatten said he would send a plane to pick him up, but Gandhi insisted on going to Delhi in a third-class railroad compartment. Their first meeting was something of a surprise for Mountbatten. "Certainly I was quite unprepared to meet such a lovable old man, with a warm, human manner; great good humour; charming manners, and perhaps most unexpectedly of all, an unfailing sense of humour. My wife and I welcomed him together, and friendly relations were effortlessly established."

Time was short. Mountbatten said, "I could sense a real tragedy round the corner if we didn't act very fast — civil war in its worst form. Beside that, Partition, much as many of us hated it, seemed a much lesser evil. I could see no alternative."

Gandhi had gone to Noakhali, in East Bengal, to stop the massacres. When he heard of the mass killings — and arson, rape, and religious atrocities — he said he would go there and die to stop the killing of Hindus by Muslims. He tramped from village to village, calming the people.

Lord Louis Mountbatten and Edwina Mountbatten invited Gandhi to tea on the lawn of the viceroy's house. After three centuries of British rule, Lord Louis had come to India to preside over a rapid transition to independence for a fifth of the world's population. Gandhi held no official position, yet he was the architect of the downfall of Empire, and Mountbatten recognized that only Gandhiji held the key to a peaceful changeover. He came to regard Gandhi as the greatest person he'd ever met: "His life was one of truth, toleration and love. . . . India, indeed the world, will not see the likes of him again, perhaps, for centuries."

Partition was inevitable. And inevitably, this also meant dividing two important regions with large Muslim populations, Bengal in the west and the Punjab in the east.

Working around the clock, Mountbatten's team produced an Independence Plan in six weeks. Jinnah was not enthusiastic about it. Although he had insisted on Partition, he wasn't satisfied with what he called his "moth-eaten Pakistan." The main argument was over the two key provinces in Northern India, Bengal and the Punjab. Jinnah had insisted on Partition — otherwise the Muslims would be swamped in Hindu India. Mountbatten and Congress said, "By the same argument, the two provinces you want in Pakistan, with large non-Muslim minorities, will also have to be partitioned."

Independence, when it came, came fast. Many said too fast. Most of the princes were persuaded, cajoled, bribed, or frightened into joining the new Indian States. Pakistan became two parts, separated by more than eight hundred miles. A great deal has happened since then. The eastern part of Pakistan,

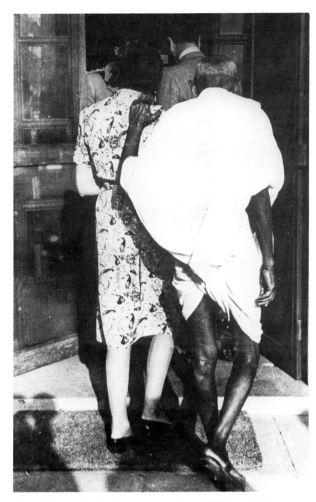

Gandhi and Lady Edwina enter the viceroy's house for the negotiations. It was a heartbreaking time for Gandhi, as he tried to prevent partitioning India into separate Hindu and Muslim countries. After thirty years of work, he was willing to postpone independence to keep India united. But he lost, as mounting violence forced Mountbatten to accept the split.

East Bengal, broke away in 1971 and became Bangladesh.

Partition

For many of India's people, August 15, 1947, was one of the greatest days in history. One-fifth of the population of the world gained independence that day. All the quarrels and animosities that had built up between the Indians and the British over the decades seemed to melt away. There was great rejoicing.

But Gandhi found nothing to celebrate. He felt "partition of the heart." "My independence," he said,

51

August 15, 1947:
Independence Day at the
Red Fort in Delhi. Even
though Gandhi had
devoted forty years of his
life to lead the Indian
people to independence,
he would not attend the
ceremony. He was in
Calcutta fasting and
working for peace
between violent Hindu
and Muslim groups.

"has not yet come. There is no reason for festivals and merriments like this." Gandhi's ideal of unity, for which he had fought all his life, had been rejected. He felt deserted by his fellow countrymen, abandoned by loved colleagues and friends.

Gandhi had always said he would like to live to be 125 years old. Now, as the violence mounted and Hindus and Muslims started to kill each other, he said at his prayer meetings, "I wanted to be 125. Now I have lost interest in life." But even in these last months of his life, Gandhi still had more great battles to fight.

"The old man has done it again"

August 1947 found Gandhi in Calcutta. Feeling sad and rejected himself, Gandhi could still bring courage, comfort, and forgiveness to others. Calcutta had already been through a year of terrible violence before Gandhi arrived. A well known Indian writer,

Sudhin Datta, remembered later, "For a year it had seemed as if it was not worth living in Calcutta. And then Gandhi had come. The first day I think they threw brickbats at him and sticks at him, and then of course he talked to them and slowly, in two or three days, the atmosphere changed and on the fourteenth what we saw is perhaps the only miracle I have seen in my life."

The "miracle" was Muslims and Hindus dancing and celebrating together and soldiers with little flags on their bayonets pinned on by the crowd. Everybody said, "The old man has done it again!"

Still Gandhi could not celebrate. By the end of the month, violence again erupted and Gandhi himself just escaped injury. He told the people he would start a fast to the death in Calcutta, to end only when the violence ended. Within four days, the chief citizens of Calcutta brought him written promises of peace by their peoples, and Gandhi was able to break his fast.

Twelve million people fled in opposite directions, as Muslims left India for the newly created country of Pakistan, and Hindus fled Pakistan for India. (See map on page 62.) Over half-a-million people died in communal violence. This picture was a reconstruction of the exodus taken for the film Gandhi.

One-man boundary force

That was in Bengal. In the Punjab, in the north, where the authorities had also expected riots, fifty-five thousand soldiers were stationed. They were overwhelmed by the violence and by the number of people who were forced to leave their homes. Then Gandhi arrived. As Mountbatten said later, "When the trouble started, the 55,000-man boundary force in the Punjab was swamped by riots, but my one-man boundary force brought peace in Bengal."

In September, Gandhi undertook his last journey — back to Delhi. The capital city was ablaze with communal strife. There was murder and bloodshed. Refugees were fleeing from the old walled city as others were pouring in. This was just a small part of the mass movement of peoples taking place all over northern India. No one really knows how many lives were lost in these tragic weeks of violence, but a figure of 200 thousand killed is probably too low!

The British viceroy, Lord Mountbatten, called Gandhi his "one man boundary force." Thousands of troops could not stop the violence in East Bengal — but Gandhi did. He walked through mud and swamps to preach his method of nonviolence. And everywhere he went he brought peace.

More than *fifteen million* fled from India to Pakistan or in the opposite direction.

Gandhi set to work. "I must do what I can to calm the heated atmosphere," he said. He visited the refugee camps. Some housed Sikhs and Hindus driven out of the Punjab; some contained Muslims chased out of their homes in Delhi. His platform was the daily prayer meeting, which was usually held in the garden of Birla House where he was staying. His preaching and readings from the Hindu Bhagavad-Gita, the Muslim Koran and the Jewish-Christian Bible were an inspiration. Hundreds attended. Often thousands more listened on the radio.

The last fast

Prayer was not enough. Gandhi felt he must do more. In January 1948, he announced his intention to begin a fast to the death. "The fast will end," he said, "when I am satisfied that there is a reunion of hearts of all communities." This, at the age of seventy-eight, was to be his eighteenth great fast, the final fast of his life.

By the third day of the fast, the Indian government was persuaded by Gandhi to make a considerable payment of money due to Pakistan. Many Hindus were outraged. They thought Gandhi was fasting to assist the Muslims who were at war with India in Kashmir. Crowds of refugee Sikhs and Hindus demonstrated outside Birla House, chanting "Blood for Blood" and "Let Gandhi die."

Gandhi was finally satisfied by the pledges given to him by the leaders of the different communities in Delhi. These representatives promised to restore communal peace and friendship by every possible effort, even at the cost of their own lives. Gandhi broke his fast on the sixth day.

Gandhi did not spare himself. Without allowing himself time to recover from the fast, he went back to work. He was now working furiously on plans to give power to the people and on many of his old ideas about putting life back into the villages. In the

Three dead bodies lie unattended and unnoticed in the streets of Calcutta. Approximately three thousand people — mainly Muslims — had died during the previous five-day clash. Calcutta was the scene of the most violent clashes both before and during independence. It was only Gandhi who was able to calm Calcutta, and then only by another fast to the death. Yet again, he very nearly died. Yet again, he achieved his objective.

Gandhi with his two great-nieces, Manu and Abhu. He called them "my walking sticks." They had cared for him since Kasturba's death. This photograph was taken the day before Gandhi's assassination. He was only just able to walk, as he was recovering from the fast that had brought peace to the Delhi mobs.

evenings, he held the usual prayer meetings. At one of these, shortly after Gandhi broke his fast, a bomb was thrown. It injured nobody. But Sardar Patel, the Minister of Home Affairs, was fearful that Gandhi would be killed. He wanted everyone attending the prayer meetings to be searched. Gandhi refused.

"If I have to die, I should like to die at the prayer meeting. You are wrong in believing that you can protect me from harm. God is my Protector," Gandhi told Patel.

The death of Gandhi

When Gandhi was fighting for Indian rights in South Africa, he was attacked by fellow Indians. One Muslim Indian who suspected him of betraying the cause threatened to kill him. Gandhi was not dismayed, because death held no fear for him. At that time, Gandhi had said, "Death is the appointed end of all life. To die by the hand of a brother rather than by a disease . . . cannot be for me a matter of sorrow and if I am free from thought of anger or hatred against my assailant I know that will rebound to my eternal welfare."

And so, forty years later it was to be.

Gandhi's thoughts about death were Hindu thoughts. He did not believe in a personal meeting with God. In fact he believed the self, the individual person, would disappear. He thought of death as the joining of streams and rivers to the sea.

On the last day of his life, Gandhi rose in the cold, clear Delhi dawn at three o'clock in the morning. Most of the day he worked, held meetings, and spent time in prayer. He was still at Birla House where he had entered on his final fast.

At about five o'clock that evening, after a meeting with Patel, Gandhi hurried from the house because he was late for evening prayers. Robert Stimson, a British correspondent who was there, tells us, "He was wearing his usual white loincloth and a pair of sandals. He had thrown a shawl around his chest, for it was getting chilly. His arms were resting lightly on the shoulders of two companions and he was smiling. There were only two or three hundred people in the

garden, and they pressed eagerly towards him as he climbed the steps leading to the small raised lawn where the congregation had gathered. As he got to the top of the steps and approached the crowd, he took his arms from the shoulders of his friends and raised his hands in salutation. He was still smiling. A thick-set man, in his thirties, I should say, and dressed in khaki, was in the forefront of the crowd. He moved a step towards Mr. Gandhi, took out a revolver, and fired several shots."

Gandhi murmured "Hey Ram" (Oh God), stood for just a few seconds, blood seeping into his white clothes, and at once fell down.

He was dead.

Lord Mountbatten remarked some years later what it was like to receive the news of Gandhi's death: "I was absolutely numbed and petrified. I went round at once to Birla House. There was a large crowd around the house already and inside it most of the members of government — everyone in tears. Gandhi looked peaceful in death, but I dreaded what

Each evening while he was in New Delhi, Gandhi would leave his quarters at Birla House to conduct evening prayers in the garden. On January 30, 1948, he was assassinated on his way to the waiting crowd. This photograph is from the film Gandhi. *The picture opposite is the actual scene of the Mahatma, with his greatnieces, on January 29, the day before his death.*

57

सच पर विश्वास रखो
सच ही सोचो सच ही करो
BELIEVE IN TRUTH
THINK TRUTH &
LIVE TRUTH

A statue of Mahatma Gandhi in Delhi. In towns and villages thoroughout India there are statues in memory of the Mahatma. The inscription reads, "Believe in truth, think truth, and live truth."

his death might bring.

"As I went into the house where his body was lying, someone in the crowd shouted, 'It was a Muslim who did it!' I turned, and said, 'You fool, don't you know it was a Hindu?'

"Of course I didn't know — no one knew at that stage. But I did know this, if it was a Muslim, we were lost. There would be civil war without fail. Thank God it wasn't."

It turned out to be a mad Hindu extremist — a young man frrom Poona, named Nathuram Godse, who was later hanged, along with another conspirator. Five others were sentenced to life imprisonment. Gandhi's funeral took place on the banks of the holy river Jumna, at Rajghat, where a million people stood waiting for the funeral procession. Ramadas set fire to his father's funeral pyre, which burned for fourteen hours. Gandhi's ashes were then scattered in the sacred rivers of India and in the sea at Bombay.

Prime Minister Nehru, speaking on the radio, gave news of Gandhi's death to the Indian people shortly after the murder: "The light has gone out of our lives, and there is darkness everywhere, and I do not know what to tell you and how to say it. Our beloved leader, Bapu as we call him, the Father of our Nation, is now no more."

Gandhi's gifts to India and the world

Later, Nehru was to remark, "'The light has gone out,' I said, and yet I was wrong. For the light that shone in this country was no ordinary light. The light that has illuminated this country for this many years will illumine this country for many more years, and a thousand years later that light will be seen in this country, and the world will see it, and it will give solace to innumerable hearts. For that light represented the living truth, and the eternal man was with us with his eternal truth reminding us of the right path, drawing us from error, taking this ancient country to freedom."

This surely is the point about Gandhiji. He was a beacon of sanity in an insane world. His was the light of reason. His was the voice of love, tolerance, and peace in this century of ultimate violence.

The little man in the loincloth left behind far more than his modest possessions: his wire spectacles, his sandals, his nickle-plated watch, his walking stick, and his twopenny Chinese monkeys.

If it is true that the evil that men do lives after them then so, surely, does the good. The problem is we can't measure it. We can't bottle wisdom. We can't package compassion. We can't measure love

Gandhi's personal belongings reflected his belief in nonpossession. These were a few of the items he used at the time of his death: chappals *(wooden sandals), a cheap nickel-plated watch, Chinese monkeys (symbolizing "Speak no evil, see no evil, hear no evil"), spectacles, a bowl, a spoon and a book of songs.*

with a tape measure.

The poor man's friend

What then are we to make of the modest little man with a genius for making the headlines? The poor man's friend? Definitely. A bit of a saint perhaps? That too. And at the same time, Gandhi was a smart, Western-trained lawyer, a man with great energy, a journalist, a propagandist, a politician, a pragmatist.

Gandhi's great success in many ways was to prepare his people for independence. All his life he had taught truthfulness and cleanliness. He taught the Hindus proper pride in their own culture and traditions. He taught self-respect where before, under the yoke of Empire, there had been submissiveness. By the example of his own courage and fearlessness, Gandhi taught his people to stand up for themselves.

For most of his life, and certainly in his last days, Gandhi had no official position, yet he swayed millions. He was a kind of latter-day saint. To the Hindu he belonged to a long tradition of hermit saints, holy men who renounced the world and lived in caves. Gandhi, of course, was always surrounded by friends and admirers, but he did renounce the pleasures of the world. He identified with the poor and they with him. He was loved by the factory workers, the poor peasants, and the depressed classes for whom he consistently fought. He won the affection of many Muslims for his efforts on their behalf. He came to embody the true spirit of India.

Gandhi visited the King of England at Buckingham Palace in his loin cloth. The King asked him, "Mr. Gandhi, how is India doing?" Gandhi replied, pointing to his skinny limbs and his poor loincloth, "Look at me. You will know from me what India is like." Perhaps this was the secret of Gandhi's power and his mass appeal. Many Indians looked upon him as a real symbol of India. In his poverty and his humility, he mirrored their lives. He could talk to them. He could express their thoughts. He was one of them.

"What I have been striving and pining to achieve these thirty years is to see God face to face."
Mahatma Gandhi

60

Gandhi's memorial, the Samardhi, is in Rajghat, on the outskirts of Delhi. Indians still regard him as the father of their country and their greatest leader.

"Gandhi taught the world that there are higher things than force, higher even than life itself; he proved that force had lost its . . . power."
Albert Szent-Gyrögyi, Nobel-laureate

"Gandhi lived, thought and acted, inspired by a vision of humanity evolving toward a world of peace and harmony." *Dr. Martin Luther King, Jr.*

"In years to come, Mahatma Gandhi will go down in history on a par with Buddha and Jesus Christ."
Lord Louis Mountbatten

"Whatever you do, do not deify him — that is what we have done in India — and he was too great a <u>man</u> to be deified." *Jawaharlal Nehru*

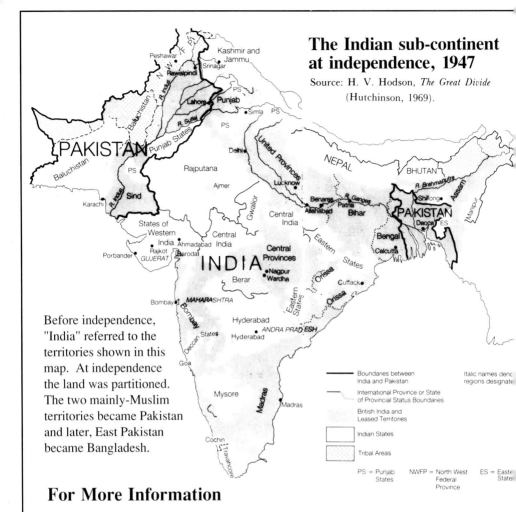

The Indian sub-continent at independence, 1947

Source: H. V. Hodson, *The Great Divide* (Hutchinson, 1969).

Before independence, "India" referred to the territories shown in this map. At independence the land was partitioned. The two mainly-Muslim territories became Pakistan and later, East Pakistan became Bangladesh.

Boundaries between India and Pakistan

International Province or State of Provincial Status Boundaries

British India and Leased Territories

Indian States

Tribal Areas

Italic names deno regions designate

PS = Punjab States   NWFP = North West Federal Province   ES = Easte State

For More Information

Organizations

The organizations listed below work to better the conditions of the people that Gandhi fought so hard to free. Write to them if you would like to know more about their work. When you write, be sure to tell them exactly what you would like to know, and include in your letter your name, address, and age.

Mother Teresa, M.C.
Missionaries of Charity
Ferrugia
54A Lower Circular Road
Calcutta 70016
India

Brother Andrew, M.C.
Missionaries of Charity Brothers
7 Mansatala Row
Kidderpore, Calcutta 70023
India

CARE
660 First Avenue
New York, NY 10016

Save the Children
54 Wilton Road
Westport, CT 06880

Catholic Relief Services
1011 First Avenue
New York, NY 10022

Lutheran World Relief
360 Park Avenue South
New York, NY 10010

Church World Service
Development Office
475 Riverside Drive
New York, NY 10115

World Vision
919 W. Huntington Drive
Monrovia, CA 91016

Books

The following books will help you learn more about Mahatma Gandhi and the people and country he loved. Check your local library or bookstore to see if they have them or can order them for you.

About Mahatma Gandhi —

Gandhi. Coolidge (Houghton Mifflin)
Gandhi. Hunter (Franklin Watts)
Gandhi's Story. Masani (Oxford)
Mahatma Gandhi. Faber (Messner)
Mahatma Gandhi: Father of Nonviolence. Peare (Hawthorn/Dutton)
Mahatma Gandhi: A Biography for Young People. Peare (Holt)
Mohandas Gandhi. Cheney (Franklin Watts)
Story of Gandhi. Shankar (Auromere)
The Story of Gandhi. Zinkin (Criterion)

About India —

Bullock Carts and Motorbikes. Roy (Atheneum)
The First Book of India. Bothwell (Franklin Watts)
Getting to Know India. Laschever (Coward/Putnam)
India. Raman (Fideler)
India: An Ancient Land, A New Nation. Sarin (Dillon)
India: Land of Rivers. Bryce (Nelson)
India: Old Land, New Nation. Watson (Garrard)
India: The Challenge of Change. Traub (Messner)
Indian Independence. Ashton (David & Charles)
India's Children. Shorter (Viking)

The Land and People of India. Modak (Lippincott)
Let's Travel in India. Geis (Childrens Press)
Let's Visit India. Caldwell (Day)
Made in India. Yaukey (Knopf)
Mother India's Children. Rice (Pantheon)
We Live in India. Sandal (Franklin Watts)
Young India. Norris (Dodd, Mead)

Glossary

Note: In Hindi pronunciation, DH is a blend of D and TH, and Rs have a kind of roll or trill at the end of the tongue.

Boer War
Fought in South Africa between the Boers, early Dutch settlers, and the British who came in the mid-1800s in search of gold. It lasted from 1899 to 1902.

Caste system
A rigid system of classes that divides into four main groups: *Brahmin*, *Kshatriya*, *Vaisya*, and *Sudra*. Each of these Hindu groups divides into thousands of smaller sub-groups that originally related to occupation or rank. But this is no longer so. There is also a large group of Untouchables, who are either of very low caste or outside the system entirely.

Congress, Indian National
Founded to let native Indians work within the government of India, it gradually became the Indians' party for agitating for independence from Britain. It originally had Muslim members as well, but it is now mostly Hindu. Since Independence in 1947, it has ruled India for all but three years.

***Dhoti* (DHOE-tee)**
Hindi word for a loincloth, a cloth that wraps around the hips.

***Durbar* (DER-BAR)**
Hindi word meaning a royal gathering for ceremonial purposes. In former times, the king held a *durbar* daily to settle disputes and make announcements.

Hindi
The national language of India, along with English. The Indian constitution recognizes fifteen other languages, among them Urdu (the official language of Pakistan) and Bengali (the official language of Bangladesh).

Hindu
A follower of Hinduism, a religion common in India and dating back to 1500 B.C.

64

Hindus follow the teachings of the Vedas, ancient texts written in Sanskrit. These texts discuss the caste system, reincarnation, and other Hindu beliefs.

Muslim
The follower of Islam, a religion founded by Mohammed, the Prophet. Muslims follow the teachings of the Koran and the Sunna, which is handed down through a collection called the Hadith. The Koran concerns what God said to Mohammed, and the Hadith concerns what Mohammed said or did in particular situations.

Pakistan
Two areas in the north of the India subcontinent where Muslims predominate. These were separated from India when India gained independence in 1947 on the insistence of the Muslims.

Wallah (WALL-ah)
Hindi suffix for someone connected to a certain movement or business or profession. A person who sells vegetables would be called a vegetable-*wallah*. If a family has been associated with a certain trade for a long time, *wallah* might become a permanent part of their name. For instance, a family doing business in silver might come to be named Chandiwallah (*chandi* meaning silver).

Chronology

1869   **October 2** — Mohandas Karamchand Gandhi born in Porbandar, India, youngest child of the Prime Minister of Porbandar.

1882   Marries Kasturba, both aged 13.

1887   Graduates from University of Bombay.

1888   First son, Harilal, is born.
September — Gandhi sails to England to pursue law degree.

1891   Passes bar exam and returns to India to practice law.

1892   Second son, Manilal, is born.

1893   **April** — Sails to Durban, South Africa, to work as a lawyer.

1894   Campaigns to uphold the right of South African Indians to vote.

1896   White South Africans attack and beat Gandhi. He begins first *satyagraba* campaign. Brings family to South Africa.

1897	Third son, Ramdas, is born.
1899	Boer War begins. Gandhi organizes Volunteer Ambulance Corps made up of Indians.
1900	Last son, Devadas, is born.
1904	Sets up first ashram, religious communal farm, for himself and his friends.
1906	The Zulu people rebel. This African tribal group lives in Natal. Gandhi again organizes ambulance corps.
1907	Gandhi leads Indians in the Transvaal in *satyagraba* campaign. They oppose government laws that require Indians to carry work permits and that make only Christian marriages legal.
1910	Establishes a second ashram, Tolstoy Farm, near Durban.
1913	South Africa recognizes Indian marriages and allows Indians to vote without paying a tax.
1915	Gandhi returns to India and founds an ashram at Ahmedabad.
1919	**March 30** and **April 6** — Gandhi calls a *hartal,* a strike. British pass the Rowlatt Act, which allows British authorities emergency powers to put down resistance in British colonies. **April 10** — Indians gather at Amritsar to demonstrate against the Rowlatt Act. The British massacre 379 and wound 1,200.
1920	Gandhi calls for nonviolent noncooperation throughout India. But violence erupts, policemen are killed, and Gandhi is jailed.
1921	The Indian National Congress gives Gandhi executive power and the right to name a successor to this position.
1922	**March 10** — Gandhi is sentenced to jail on charges of sedition.
1924	**February** — Gandhi released from jail after an appendicitis operation. For the next six years, he is less active in politics and focuses instead on establishing a sense of unity within the Indian community. **Autumn** — Gandhi fasts for three weeks to encourage people to protest through nonviolent means.
1928	Indian National Congress calls for independence for India.

1930	**March** — *Satyagraha* called for against salt tax. Gandhi leads 24-day, 241-mile Salt March to Dandi, on the seacoast. **May** — Gandhi is arrested just before Congress party organizes a demonstration at the Dharsana Salt Works.
1931	**January** — Gandhi is released from jail. He goes to London for the Round Table Conference.
1932	Gandhi returns to India, where he begins new campaign of civil disobedience and is arrested. **September** — He fasts to protest conditions for Untouchables.
1934	Gandhi resigns as leader of Congress party and Jawaharlal Nehru takes his place. Gandhi travels throughout India teaching nonviolence and arguing for the rights of the Untouchables.
1939	Gandhi again enters political life and begins the fight for Indian independence.
1942	"Quit India" resolution is passed by Congress. Gandhi and leaders resist joining Britain's side in World War II unless India is declared independent. Gandhi and leaders are arrested.
1944	**February 22** — Kasturba dies in prison. **May** — Gandhi is released from prison because of ill health.
1946	**April** — Muslims ask that Pakistan be a Muslim country.
1947	**February** — Lord Mountbatten comes to India as last English viceroy. **August 15** — Independence declared for India. The country divides into Hindu India and Muslim Pakistan. Violence erupts. **September** — Gandhi begins fast to end Hindu-Muslim violence.
1948	**January** — Gandhi fasts to bring peace to New Delhi. **January 30** — Gandhi assassinated by fanatic Hindu, Nathuram Vinayak Godse, on way to prayer meeting. United Nations General Assembly sets aside mourning period for Gandhi.

Index

DATE DUE

SE 8			
JUN 0 5 1996			
JUN 2 6 1996			

DEMCO 38-297